How To SQUAT 500 lbs. RAW

12-Week Squat Program & Technique Guide

By

Ryan J. Mathias

MathiasMethod.com

COPYRIGHT

DISCLAIMER

The information presented is meant to help guide participants through practices that can help individuals become stronger and healthier through proper use. This information, however, does not promise any benefits when misused or misinterpreted. Please follow the guidelines as directed.

When participating in any exercise or training program there is a possibility of physical injury. If you engage in any movements, exercises or training programs, you agree to do so at your own risk. By voluntarily participating in these activities, you assume all risk of injury to yourself and agree to release and discharge Mathias Method, Ryan J. Mathias and all other affiliates of any responsibility if injury occurs.

In addition, by following any of the suggested guidelines, protocols, templates, activities or any other information or advice given, you do so at your own risk. Do not begin any nutrition, health, exercise or training program without consulting with a Board Certified Medical Doctor and/or Registered Dietician first.

Always use spotters and any necessary safety equipment when training. It is your duty to inspect all training and safety equipment prior to each use.

By utilizing this information presented you are stating that you agree to our Terms of Use which can be read in full on MathiasMethod.com/terms-use/.

About The Author

Ryan J. Mathias

Hi,

I'm Ryan Mathias, creator of the Mathias Method Strength System and for years I have been helping people all over the world, from total beginners to elite athletes, learn how to get stronger, perform better, and achieve their goals.

As an athlete, Strength Coach and competitive Powerlifter with 10+ years of experience, all backed by a Degree in Exercise Science, I have taken my experience and combined it with my education to bring you the best and most effective knowledge available.

I share everything I know in my books and it is my goal to help as many people as I can learn how to achieve their goals. Because I measure my success not by how many books I sell, but by how many people I help.

So, if you want to learn how to get bigger, stronger, faster, and overall perform better, then I'm your guy!

Plus, if you ever have any questions, you can email me anytime and I will do my best to help you reach your goals!

Email: ryan@mathiasmethod.com

I would love to hear from you!

Join me on Social Media: @RyanJMathias

Books By Ryan J. Mathias

Available on

Amazon.com

and

StrengthWorld.store

Get the Official

SQUAT Shirt

and other awesome apparel at

StrengthWorld.store

Use Discount Code SQUAT500

for 20% OFF your order as a gift

for reading this book!

Dedication

This information is dedicated to you, the lifter. To those of you that believe in becoming stronger. Stronger through self-improvement and the pursuit of greater achievement. For those that always push for more and crave success every day. For those that don't let challenges stop them from doing what they set out to do. For all the dreamers out there, that keep their dreams alive!

This information is dedicated to YOU, because YOU are the only one that can make a difference in your life. YOU are the only one that can change YOUR world!

Thank You

Thank you to all those that read this information and use it to help others. My mission is to help as many people as I can change the world through strength and I know I can’t do it alone. So, thank you for standing with me.

Table Of Contents

PART 1

INTRODUCTION

A Note From The Author

Hey Lifter!

I hope you are ready to get really strong, because you are about to embark on an incredible Strength Journey! The same journey that I followed when I first started! The journey to get stronger!

For me, it all started with the dream of one day squatting over 500lbs. totally RAW! That was the very first goal I set for myself when I started weight training! I wanted to be someone that was much stronger than he looked, being that I was only 160lbs. at the time, and was able to lift tremendous weight!

As you can imagine, I have since squatted over 500 lbs. numerous times. It wouldn't make much sense for me to write this book if I hadn't. Not only have I accomplished this incredible strength feat, but I am proud to say that I have done it 100% naturally without the use of any drugs or special supplements.

I've actually been squatting 500 lbs. since I was a teenager!

However, it wasn't easy for me to get there. I had to work hard for it! Which is why I made this book. To give you an easier path to reach that almost seemingly unattainable goal of finally squatting 500+ lbs. to below parallel and somehow standing back up!

In fact, I created the entire *How To Lift More Weight* series for all the Strength Warriors out there that are just like us, looking to get stronger! I really want to help others, achieve their goals of lifting as much weight as they can dream of in all their lifts!

Just remember, it won't be easy. You are gonna have to work for it. I am giving you all the tools you need to succeed, but the rest is up to you.

Before you get started, I want you to realize that no ordinary person has ever completed this Journey. That is because in order to reach such an incredible strength feat, you cannot be ordinary. You have to develop yourself into someone that has character, focus and strength beyond the ordinary. You will have to become extraordinary in your efforts to defeat the challenging road that lays ahead.

You will have to be consistent, dedicated and self-disciplined enough to persevere to the end. You can have others join in along your journey, but YOU must be the one that keeps fighting until the end. No one can do it for you. You have to be the one that decides to not give up and push on no matter how hard it gets.

I cannot promise that you will reach your goal, but I will guarantee that this program will guide you as far as you want to go. The rest is up to you. Are you ready?

Strength To You,

Ryan J. Mathias

Go to MathiasMethod.com to learn about my Strength Journey!

The Definition of RAW

Now let's start off with a definition of what we powerlifters consider a lift to be done "RAW".

"RAW" determines the assistance you are allowed to use for training and testing your lifts. What we consider to be RAW in this book is the same as what most sanctioned Powerlifting Competitions also consider to be RAW.

This is different than what is considered to be 100% RAW. 100% RAW means without any assistive equipment at all, as if you were only lifting in shorts and a t-shirt.

For this program we allow for some safety equipment to accommodate more people and promote safety of the lifter, above all else.

To be considered RAW you can use the assistance of:

- ☑ **a weight lifting belt,**
- ☑ **non-supportive knee or elbow sleeves,**
- ☑ **chalk as needed,**
- ☑ **and wrist wraps if needed.**

**Non-supportive sleeves are used to promote joint safety by keeping the joints warm, but should add little to no actual lifting support.*

This amount of equipment promotes safety of the lifter while allowing for only necessary assistance. Overall, the lifter has to do the lift, not the equipment.

The more equipment you use, the more you have to rely on for max day. It is best to only use what you need to be safe and save the rest for when you absolutely need it.

Drugs and Supplements

Being RAW also does not allow the use of drugs or special supplement regiments that greatly improve a lifter's strength, recovery or muscle growth. Basically, if you would fail a drug test using it, then it is not RAW.

To be clear, no supplements are needed to make this program work as effectively as possible. End of story.

Lifting Equipment

Lifting equipment is anything that directly improves your ability to lift more weight. This could be very light assistive gear, such as knee or elbow sleeves, all the way up to extremely supportive gear, such as lifting suits.

One of the most common pieces of equipment to be used is a lifting belt. When used properly, a lifting belt allows you to better brace your core for stabilization by increasing the intra-abdominal pressure placed on your spine. By increasing stabilization you are enabled to lift heavier loads.

Equipment can improve lifter strength and safety, but can also have adverse effects when used improperly.

If any one piece of equipment is used too frequently, then it will limit your body's ability to grow stronger in that area. Essentially, the equipment will become a crutch that then must be used every time training occurs in order to keep up with the strength developed in other non-supported areas.

The most effective way to use equipment is only when it is necessary. For example, when using light to moderate loads (<75%) avoid using any equipment at all to build greater strength in all areas. Then when you put on equipment for maximal loads (>80%) you will be that much stronger.

Even if you have an injury, only use the equipment when you need it. If your injury does not hurt, then do not cover it up with equipment. Allow it to grow stronger.

When you are building strength, use little to no equipment.

When you are testing strength, use whatever you can to improve your lift.

The King Of All Exercises

The Squat is known as the "King of All Exercises" because it builds muscle mass throughout your entire body and tests your full body strength all in one powerful lift. The bench press and deadlift have their own place in the strength world, but having a big squat makes you King and Queen to others.

This is the lift where you are standing with weight on your shoulders that would crush an ordinary person to the ground and yet you make it bow down to you as you lift it with ease! No other lift can test your strength and will the same as the squat, and nothing can replace it.

The squat is also your base, and if you don't have a strong base to build the rest of your body on, then you will never reach your true potential.

Nobody likes the gym bro look with a huge upper body, but chicken legs to stand on. It just looks weak, like they will find any excuse to skip leg day. Don't be that person!

Build your base into the strong foundation you need to set an incredible upper body physique on! Do that and every part of your body will grow even stronger!

Though the squat focuses on your leg strength and development, your entire body must be involved to push back against the load trying to crush you where you stand. The squat helps to build muscle in all areas, including your upper body, through the releases powerful hormones. If you want bigger legs, squat. If you want bigger glutes, squat. If you want bigger arms, squat. If you want bigger anything, squat more!

All this from just one simple lift! No wonder it is called "King"!

Squat Everyday

Our bodies were designed to squat everyday! However, if we squat heavy everyday or do too much too often and don't recover from it, we are just doing more damage than good. If you do squat everyday, it needs to be at a low intensity that focuses in improving technique and aids in recovery versus tearing down more muscle.

The best way to squat everyday is with your bodyweight. This allows for a low intensity that can aid in recovery without the risk of overuse injuries or teaching improper movement patterns. You can actually greatly increase your squat strength and body function just by doing a few bodyweight squats everyday!

By simply understanding the mechanics of how to squat properly, with or without weight, you will better understand how your body was meant to function. This will enable your conscious and sub-conscious to better use all the musculature in your body properly no matter what activities you do.

With this in mind, I created the Daily 30, which is a quick everyday bodyweight exercise routine. This routine has you doing a quick 2 minute bodyweight workout at least once per day to help you practice your squatting technique, decrease muscle and joint pain, and improve your recovery between workouts. The Daily 30 will teach you how to squat more weight than ever by using the movement patterns our bodies were designed to do!

This is especially important for beginners that are still trying to perfect their squat technique, while working on improving the mobility needed to reach proper squat depth.

If you want to learn more about the Daily 30, go to my website MathiasMethod.com and start getting even stronger by squatting everyday!

Squats For Beginners

Beginners should always start any strength training exercise with their bodyweight before increasing the intensity using weights. If you cannot learn how to move properly with your own bodyweight, then adding weight is only going to make things worse and put you at a high risk of injury. Start getting stronger with your own body, then add weight when needed.

The best way to do this is simply doing the Daily 30 every single day, even after you start squatting with weight. This will ensure you are practicing your technique daily and help with any mobility issues you may have. If you have problems with knee pain, butt wink (rounding) or hitting proper depth this will correct that.

After you can do the Daily 30 with ease, it will be time to start squatting with weight and following the principles in this book.

How we teach the squat to a beginner is different than how we teach it to a more advanced lifter. This is because beginners are still figuring out their body's leverages and what works best for them while an advanced lifter knows what does and does not work for them based on experience.

When you are just starting out and discovering how your body moves with a load on its back, begin by doing what is comfortable. Grab the bar where it is comfortable, place the bar on your back where it is comfortable, stand where it is comfortable, and only go as low as you are comfortable. From there you can start making minor adjustments to see what works best for you.

Try to continuously get lower, while maintaining control of the weight and not letting the weight control you.

If you need to change something then make small changes. Remember, small changes make a big difference. So do not go from a close stance to a stance that is 6 inches wider. Start with 1 inch, then two and so on if needed.

Realize that things are going to take some time. Just be patient and soon enough you will be squatting like a pro!

Overall, beginners should focus on the basics and getting the general movement down before trying to apply every detail. The details will come. After squatting for a while you'll start to feel what works better for you versus someone else, and as your body changes, so will your technique. Focus on strength first, and improve your technique over time.

Squats For Advanced Lifters

Advanced lifters are those that have been squatting for over a year and developed a strong base of strength. If you have not been squatting for at least this long, I highly recommend you start with my *Base Of Strength Program* (see page 6) to build up all 3 of your base lifts while getting a lot of squat practice in.

Also, any beginners you know should start off with that program before advancing to the advanced program in this squat book.

An advanced lifter should be specific and focus on the details while their subconscious does the most basic aspects of the lift for them. This means taking a quick moment before every single squat to go through a checklist of specifics you need to perfect your squat.

Squat Checklist

After you set-up and walk the weight out, take a quick moment to check:

- ☑ **Are your feet grabbing the ground?**
- ☑ **Are your knees twisting out?**
- ☑ **Are your glutes flexed?**
- ☑ **Is your core braced; front, back and sides?**
- ☑ **Are you pulling the bar into you?**
- ☑ **Are you driving your head back into the bar?**
- ☑ **Are you confident and focused on your lift?**

If you can answer "Yes" to all of these questions, then you are perfectly set to squat big. The next step is to perfect your lifting technique.

The squat is a lift that is never perfect and needs constant tweaking. You can always move smoother. You can always drive harder. You can always brace tighter. There is always something to improve and focus on.

With every workout, try to focus on one or two aspects of your technique to improve on. If you need help, asking a knowledgeable friend or trainer can really help. They can give you feedback both during your set and immediately after to help you see what needs to improve.

If you don't have that option, you can always record yourself. Just try to video from multiple angles to make sure no technique issues are hiding from the camera angle you chose.

You can also ask me anytime! You can tag me on Instagram @MathiasMethod or Facebook @MathiasMethodStrength asking for some tips and I would be happy to take a look at your lifts!

If we don't get back to you within day, then you can always message us or try my personal account @RyanJMathias. I am active on all accounts daily, but I am also a busy guy. I will get to as many as I can as often as I can, so please be patient with me if the response is not immediate.

Just remember, your squat is NEVER going to be perfect! There is always something to improve! If you are not improving, then you are limiting your full potential.

Now let's find what you need to improve and go squat!

Squat Principles

All proper squat technique will have the same principles, no matter your stance or bar position, that must be followed for safe and effective technique. These principles are presented below.

- ☑ **The bar travels straight up and down over your center of gravity (mid-foot).**
- ☑ **Hips drop below top of the knees for full range of motion.**
- ☑ **Back flat with a neutral spine; no rounding or arching.**
- ☑ **Knees and hips move simultaneously.**
- ☑ **Knees travel in line with the toes.**
- ☑ **Feet stay locked into the ground.**

These Squat Principles apply to all squats.

Any squat that follows these principles is a perfect squat! Speed is not important. Technique and control of the weight is.

To perfect these squatting principles, get my book *The Daily 30* which has taken, not only my squat, but all my lifts to a whole new level just by practicing my technique daily!

Beyond these principles, there are two main variables that can change how a squat looks and is used. These are squat stance and bar position.

Choosing Your Squat Stance

Generally, a closer stance utilizes greater knee flexion focusing the tension on your quads, while a wider stance utilizes more hip flexion, or torso lean, and puts the tension on your lower back and glutes.

Greater knee flexion better emphasizes quadriceps use while more hip flexion emphasizes more glute and hamstring use.

Choose the stance that best utilizes your leverages.

If you have strong legs (quads), you may want to try a close stance with your toes turned out a bit. If you have a strong lower back and hips (glutes), then you may prefer a wider stance with toes pointed more straight ahead.

Note: *For beginners, just stand where it feels comfortable and adjust from there as your technique develops.*

Choosing Your Bar Placement

A higher bar position normally allows for less torso lean and more knee flexion while a lower bar position allows for greater torso lean and more posterior chain muscles utilization.

If you are quad dominant and have a lot of knee flexion in your squat, you may want to choose the high bar position to help keep a more upright torso. This will allow the energy to transfer better from the ground into the bar and puts more of the tension on your legs to squat the weight up.

If you have a wide stance and tend to be stronger when you use your hips more by leaning over in the squat, you may want to try a low bar position. This puts more of the tension into your hips, and works with your strength.

Note: *For beginners, just place the bar in the most comfortable spot or in the middle of your Upper Trapezius. You can adjust from there over time.*

PART 2

PERFECTING YOUR TECHNIQUE

Squat Technique Guide

The Ultimate Squat Guide

This one-of-a-kind Squat Guide gives you all the tools you need to squat more weight than ever!

- ☑ **Breathing and Bracing Techniques**
- ☑ **Proper Set-Up**
- ☑ **How To Unrack**
- ☑ **Proper Lifting Technique**
- ☑ **Technique Checklist**
- ☑ **Common Mistakes and How To Correct Them**
- ☑ **Top Accessory Exercises**
- ☑ **Squat Variations**
- ☑ **How To Box Squat**
- ☑ **Tips and Tricks**
- ☑ **and even How To Spot Properly**

Read on to start building your strongest squat ever!

SQUAT

PURPOSE

- **Test Lower Body Strength**
- **Build Leg and Core Strength**

PRIME MOVERS

- **Quadriceps** (Legs)
- **Hamstrings** (Legs)
- **Glutes** (Hips)

Breathing and Bracing

How you breathe during your squats can greatly influence how the squat is performed and your maximal strength. What you may have been taught before is to breathe in as you descend during a lift and breathe out as you stand back up. This is good if you are in a cardio class using extremely light weights, and just need to keep your endurance up, but if you are looking to get stronger this is one of the worst things you can do.

By breathing in as you descend, your body is not as tight as it can be, and is, therefore, unstable. It is similar to doing a squat on an exercise ball versus squatting on the ground. The more stable you are, the more you can lift. So you need to think more about how you are going to breathe during your squats than what people do for general fitness.

If you want to get stronger, or build muscle, then you need to lift heavy, and to lift heavy you need to have your body braced as tightly as possible to have the most strength for your lift. For that you should use what is called the Valsalva Maneuver, which promotes the greatest amount of strength by increasing your spine stabilization through increased intra-abdominal pressure. The two versions of this are described next.

Valsalva Maneuver

Suck in as much air as you can and hold it in, attempting to create as much intra-abdominal pressure as you can, to stabilize your spine. Then press your lips closed to hold the air in while flexing all of the musculature surrounding your entire torso, and forcing the air deep down into your abdomen.

Think of your torso as a soda can you are trying to fill up and pressurize. You have your pelvic floor as the base, your diaphragm as the top, and all your abdominal (front, back and side) musculature making the outer walls of the can. You want to fill the can with air and flex everything around it as tight as possible to keep the air in.

Your lifting belt can help with this, but make sure that you do not tighten it too much or your will put a dent in the can, and if you dent a can even slightly, the can crushes. Always keep your belt loose enough so that you can put the just the 4 fingers of your hand down into the belt against your stomach with ease. Then when you brace you want to think of bracing out against the belt so that it gets filled up tightly and your fingers can no longer fit in.

The valsalva maneuver greatly increases your blood pressure and should only be held for 1-2 maximal repetitions, or when you are using over 90% of your maximum. Sets with more than 1-3 reps, or under 90% of your maximum should use the Partial Valsalva Maneuver.

Partial Valsalva Maneuver

This is the same as the Valsalva Maneuver, except you exhale after getting past the sticking point of the lift. This helps to decrease the overall blood pressure increase created by the pressure and allows for more fluid reps to be performed, while still having a very strong lift.

For the squat, start to breathe out, while still bracing your core, after you have made it about half way up from the bottom of the squat. Then breathe in again before every rep to re-brace.

Set-Up

Your squat set-up is all about creating tension in the right places without wasting energy. You need to maintain that same tightness during your entire squat. If you lose tightness then you lose strength.

Grab The Bar

Grasp bar firmly, with thumbs wrapped, as close to your shoulders as you can while maintaining a relatively neutral wrist position, that allows you to still pull the bar into your body.

If you grab too wide, then you will lose back tightness and risk falling out of position. If you grab too close, then you can stress your wrists and will be pushing the bar off your back rather than creating tightness from it.

Find the best position for you, and if you have shoulder or wrist mobility problems you should try to improve them before every training session. You can do this with my *How To Warm-Up Properly For Strength Training Guide* (See page 6).

Set Your Feet Directly Under The Bar

Set your feet directly under the bar in your squat stance so that the bar is directly over your mid foot.

If you set your feet behind the bar, then you will waste valuable energy as you have to pull the weight out of the rack from in front of your center of gravity.

You want to be able to stand straight up with the weight and not be out of position.

Set The Bar On Your Back

Squat down and place the bar in the strongest position for you on your upper back, anywhere between the base of your neck and middle of rear deltoids (shoulder muscle).

Note: *A higher bar position will emphasize greater knee flexion and less torso lean, while a lower bar position will emphasize more torso lean and less knee flexion.*

Unrack

Brace Your Core

Suck in as much air as you can and hold it in, attempting to create as much intra-abdominal pressure as you can, to stabilize your spine. Then press your lips closed to hold the air in while flexing all of the musculature surrounding your entire torso, and forcing the air deep down into your abdomen. This is known as the Valsalva Maneuver.

Hold this tightness throughout your entire set-up.

Pull The Bar Into You

Pull your elbows down and in towards your hips throughout the movement, as if you are going to bend the bar over your back. This keeps that bar locked in and it should never, ever slide out of place, if done properly.

Push Your Head Back Into The Bar

While keeping a neutral spine, force your head back into the bar, with your eyes straight ahead. Imagine pulling your chin straight back, and never tilt your head up.

Maintain a neutral head position (straight spine) throughout the entire lift with eyes straight ahead.

Stand Straight Up With The Weight

Flex your glutes hard as you simultaneously, extend your knees and hips to lift the bar straight up, just over the rack hooks. Stay tight while you do this.

Walk It Out

Slide one foot at a time back 3-4 inches, or just enough to clear the rack hooks, so you are standing in your squat stance.

The farther you move the more likely you are to be out of position and waste energy. The bar should move straight up and down when you squat, so you do not need to move back very far.

The Squat

Foot Position

Toes should point somewhere between 10-45 degrees out depending on your stance width and mobility. Try different positions and see what works best for you.

If your heels come up as you squat or you have trouble getting to depth, then try either turning your toes out more or widening your stance, until you improve your ankle mobility.

Grab The Ground

Suction cup your feet to the ground by spreading your toes as wide as you can, then grasping the floor with your entire foot. Your entire foot (heel, ball of your foot, and outer edge) should stay locked into the ground.

Then, while clenching your toes into the ground like eagle claws, create torque by externally rotate your feet, as if they were to spin in place, throughout the entire motion.

This movement should flex your entire lower body from your glutes down through your entire legs so that everything is tight, and nothing is loose or relaxed.

Maintain this external rotation torque throughout the lift.

Note: *By grabbing the ground with your foot you are simply creating a strong arch in your foot, not rolling your ankle. Your feet should not move out of place or come up at all during these motions. Just create a rotational pressure to stabilize your joints, while your entire foot is locked into the ground.*

Re-Brace Your Core

While keeping your entire body tight, again suck in as much air as you can and press it down deep into your abdomen increasing the intra-abdominal pressure. Hold this tightness throughout the entire lift.

Bend At The Hip

Initiate the motion by bending at the waist, pushing your hips back slightly, maintaining a neutral spine as if doing a 3 inch bow. This is a slight motion just to open the hips.

The weight should stay over your mid foot, with no back arching.

Push Your Knees Out

Push your knees out laterally to open your hips throughout the lift. This better engages your hips and makes for a stronger squat.

Your knees should travel in line with your toes during the entire lift. If they cave in at all then you need to work on your glute strength AND adductor mobility (inner thigh - being able to do the splits better to open up your hips).

Squat Straight Down and Up

While maintaining a neutral spine, open your hips and descending straight down into a full depth squat, bending your knees and hips simultaneously, then forcefully press back up into the bar as you ascend, by extending your hips and knees together.

Keep your head neutral and knees pressed out over your foot.

If you set-up properly your body should do most of the movement for you. All you have to do is go straight down and back up with force.

SIDE VIEW

Key Points

- ☑ Stay tight throughout the entire set-up and squat.
- ☑ Pull the bar into you.
- ☑ Grab the ground with your feet.
- ☑ Torque your knees out throughout the full range of motion.
- ☑ Control the lift with your glutes.
- ☑ Maintain a neutral spine and head position.
- ☑ Drive back up into the bar to stand.

Always use spotters during your squats for safety.

Common Squat Mistakes

Improper set-up

Make sure that everything is perfect before you start. If you set-up wrong, then your entire lift is going to be wrong.

You can't correct your position while lifting so you have to make it perfect before you even take the weight off the rack.

When you set-up, make sure to take your time. Don't rush it. Even if you have to do your entire set-up multiple times, it is best to take that few extra seconds to get yourself in the best position to lift from, then rush it and risk missing a lift or getting injured.

Your set-up should be exactly the same every single time so that you are always lifting from the same perfect position and not just lazily going through the motions. If you want to lift big weight, then you need to take the time to perfect everything, including your set-up.

Grabbing the bar too close or too wide

Where you place your hands matters, because it effects how well you can transfer energy from you into the bar. When you are in perfect position your hands should be placed to where you can best pull the bar into your back to create even more tightness throughout your entire body. This makes you in control of the bar rather than letting the bar control you. If you bar moves at all, you are not in control.

By grabbing the bar too wide, you are losing pulling power to where the bar is just sitting on you rather than attached to your back. If you have shoulder problems that prevent you from getting your hands in closer, then check out my Mobility Exercises to work on improving your shoulder mobility and make sure you to follow my How To Warm-Up Guide to help decrease pain and increase mobility before every workout.

By grabbing the bar too close, your hands will be getting crushed by the weight and naturally start pushing back up against the weight to get it off of you. Not only that, but you put your shoulders and wrists in compromised positions which can lead to impingement and joint problems. Make sure that you grab wide enough to where you can still pull the bar into you and not cause joint pain.

Turning toes out too much

This is a common mistake for many squatters that are taught they get more power by having their toes turned out when squatting. It is true that turning your toes out helps to engage the glutes better in squats. However, many people take it too far.

If you turn your toes out more than 45 degrees you actually decrease the amount of power you can get from your glutes by shortening the muscle too much. Muscle's are strongest in their mid-range of motion and lose power near full extension and full contraction. For the glutes you will get the most power by turning your toes out only 10-30 degrees depending upon your stance and mobility.

Generally with a wider stance your toes should be fairly straight ahead and with a close stance they should be turned out more. This is due to ankle mobility mostly. If you have tight ankles, turning your toes out can help hide this mobility issue, but it still needs to be worked on. A tight muscle is not a strong muscle.

Tilting your head back

Your body follows your head, meaning that if you if you arch your head back, then your entire spine naturally arches with it, and if you tuck your head forward, then your entire spine rounds forward. That is why head position is so important during all of your lifts, especially the squat.

To put your back in the strongest position, it needs to be neutral, or flat. Not arched or rounded. Arching and rounding puts a lot of unnecessary strain on your spinal column and leads to back problems that you do not want. However, if you keep a flat back, or as flat as you can make it, during your lifts, then your back will be totally safe from harm.

This all starts with your head position. You should try to keep your eyes focused straight in front of you as you lift and drive your head back, as if pulling your chin back towards your neck.

DO NOT LOOK UP! Look straight ahead!

Standing too wide or too close

Just like you can stand to close, you can stand too wide. If your stance is too narrow or too wide, then you will lose power and risk injury.

Your stance should never be so close that you cannot reach proper depth or to where your ankles start to raise at the bottom of the squat. This puts a lot of strain on your knees and ankles, and takes your hips out of optimal position.

Your stance should also never be so wide that you cannot push your knees out over your ankles in the bottom position. You should stand no wider than where your knees are the same width apart at the base of your squat as your feet are. By standing too wide you will put a lot of strain on your knees, ankles and hips, which is just asking for injury. If you need to, work on improving your (inner thigh) hip adductor mobility.

Butt-wink

Butt-wink is where your pelvis rotates backwards at the bottom of your squat and looks as if you are tucking your tailbone underneath you. This is not a major issue, unless it is causing back pain, and most people don't even know that they are doing it. All it means is that you have tight, or short, hamstrings that are reaching their full extension in the bottom position of your squat. So all you have to do to fix this is improve the flexibility of your hamstrings, which can also make them stronger and relieve any back pain you may have.

Going too Low

Many people don't actually see this as a problem, but when it comes to strength, every inch matters. If you increase the range of motion of any of your lifts you have to be that much stronger just to go that extra distance.

For those that have a close stance, there is a large range of motion and it can even be to the point of where you are stronger by going lower, because you can bounce your hamstrings off of your calves to give you a little boost out of the bottom. There is nothing majorly wrong with this, but if you are going more than just a few inches below parallel, the overall boost is not going to be enough to make up for those inches when you have over 400 pounds on your back.

For wide stance squatters this can be really damaging to your knees and hips. So, pay attention to depth. You do not want to go so low that your knees are caving in and hips are getting pinched. Control the entire movement and as soon as you hit depth, drive back up hard.

Not going low enough

This is probably the most common mistake most people make with the squat. Whether you are a gym bro, a bodybuilder or a powerlifter, it is NEVER correct to consider a partial squat as a full squat. There is a place for partial range of motion, but building complete squat strength and leg development does not come from partial squats. Full range of motion is necessary for complete muscle growth and overall strength.

With that being said, it is really not that big of a deal if someone doing general fitness does a half squat or bodybuilders stop a few inches above parallel. Unless you are competing for something that demands perfect form, who really cares? You do you. Let them do their thing.

Proper depth for any squat variation is where your hip crease goes below the top of your knee. That means, where the front top of your shorts folds over as you lower into a squat should go below the top part of your knee cap on every rep. Don't base depth on the top of your thigh being parallel to the floor, because as your thighs get bigger this gets harder and your squat stance changes how your thigh is positioned for this. It should always be based on your hip going below your knee.

Overall, just use your best judgement. If you question wether you went low enough or not, then you did not go low enough. There should be no question about proper depth if you go low enough. I always say, "go one inch lower than you want too" and you will always be correct.

If you have mobility issues that prevent you from going that low, then you should work on your hip and ankle mobility. More often than not, it is actually your ankles that are tight and preventing you from hitting proper depth.

Also get my book *The Daily 30* (see page 6) to work on your squat technique and mobility daily for the best results.

Looking in the mirror while you squat

Yes, looking in the mirror is a problem. It is ok to do every once in a while to check your technique with light weight, but you should not rely on watching yourself squat every time you lift. You need to be able to feel how your body moves and not just watch it.

Think and feel. Think of what you should be feeling, and feel it. If you watch yourself, we tend to get side tracked and only watch certain things. You need to get comfortable squatting without a mirror, and if all the squat racks are in front of mirrors, then try to ignore it and just stare into your own eyes rather than looking all around.

This is especially important for those of you looking to compete in powerlifting. In powerlifting, there are no mirrors on the platform and you will be facing a huge crowd of people in front of you. This can throw some people off if they are not used to it, so make sure you practice feeling your squats and looking off into the distance.

DO NOT set-up in a rack backwards to fix this problem. That is unsafe and just dumb.

Neglecting your hips

The squat is a combination of a knee bend AND a Hip Hinge movement. A Hip Hinge is where you bend at the hips, the same as doing a bow, then stand back up.

Your back should not do any of this movement. It is simply a stabilizer that allows you to lift the weight with a neutral spine.

Though this is all true, many people are afraid of putting any stress on their back for fear of injury. Instead they try not to bend over at all and put all the stress on the knee and ankle joint, which is not made to take the entire load without the support of the hips.

When you squat YOU NEED TO USE YOUR HIPS and legs together! They both support each other during the movement and make big squats possible. If you neglect one, then the other takes all the stress without any support leading to injury.

So, put your hips into it! The Hip Hinge is one of the strongest motions the human body was designed to do and needs to be used for proper squat technique. Simply set the weight into your hips when you squat down and then drive them forward as you stand. This is both safe and correct.

Top Accessory Exercises

The best lift to build up your squat is the squat. That is the same for any lift. However, you can only squat so much and so often before you start overdoing it to where the benefits plateau. That is where accessory exercises come into play.

Accessory exercises allow you to get in more training volume and help to build up specific muscle groups that may need more direct attention.

For example, you can use front squats to build up quad strength or glute-ham raises to build up hamstring strength.

These are the best accessory exercises to increase your squat:

- **Squat Variations** for different leg stimulus.
- **Front Squats** or **Leg Press** for quad strength.
- **Deadlifts** for hip, hamstring, core and back strength.
- **Glute-Ham Raises** for hamstring strength.
- **Good Mornings** for hip and core strength.
- **Weighted planks** for core strength.
- **Plyometric Jumps** for maximal strength and explosive power.

There are thousands of other exercises that can help build up your strength for squats, but these are the most effective ones that have a direct carry-over to your squat strength. Improve these, and your squat strength will absolutely go up.

These are also the accessory exercises you will be doing in any of of my Mathias Method Strength Programs, including the 12-Week Squat Program in this book!

These exercises are hard, but they are also highly effective in building full body strength like nothing else can. Work these often and your strength will shoot up!

Squat Variations

Lift variations allow for a different stimulus and can allow for new growth, building up specific parts of the lift. This is also a great way to target specific muscle groups that may be lagging behind and need more attention.

Variation can be simple or complex, but to build strength towards the main movements, it is important not to vary too far from the original lift. Start with simple variations before moving into more complex changes.

It doesn't make sense to vary the lift so drastically to where it is a completely different lift that may not have any carryover to your actual squat.

Here are some Common Variations you can use to spice up your lifts:

- **Stance or Grip**
- **Bar Positioning**
- **Pauses**
- **Boxes or Boards**
- **Specialty Bars**
- **Range of Motion**
- **Accommodating Resistance (Bands or Chains)**
- **Assistive Gear**

Variation is a great way to spice up your training, but needs to be limited. If you truly want to build a lot of strength, then you need to put in the work and not just find ways to make lifts easier.

Variation is best used with advanced lifters who have already mastered their lifting technique and progress is stalling. Beginners should rarely use variations in the main lifts if at all, because the best variation to build up your squat is just doing more squats. It is only after standard squats are not working well that you should try something different.

Intermediate lifters can try some exercise variations infrequently, but most of the work should focus on perfecting the main lift.

How To Box Squat

The Box Squat is one of the most commonly used variations to the squat. It utilizes a box to teach squat technique, decrease the stress of heavy squatting and build strength at specific depths.

The box breaks the squat into 3 parts so that you can focus on perfecting each part of the lift separately.

1. **The Descent -** By descending under control onto the box you will learn to better control the descent of a squat.

2. **The Pause -** Pausing on the box allows you to ensure that your body stays tight at the bottom of the squat and builds strength at that specific depth.

3. **The Lift -** To come off the box you must use more force than normal by exploding up with your hips and legs in unison building explosive strength.

The box squat is simply the best way to perfect your squat form while building strength, other than performing more squats.

Your deload weeks are a great time to work on your box squat and advanced lifters can use it for their main lift on Base Work sessions to take off some stress from the intense weights.

The Box

Use a box that is strong enough to withstand the weight you are going to put onto it during your squat. Also, make sure that the box is not going to wobble or slide when you sit onto it.

The box height can vary based upon your goals and mobility. If you lack the mobility to sit onto a parallel box with proper form, then start at a height about 1 inch below where you can maintain form and lower the box height 1 inch every 2-3 weeks as your mobility improves. This will help build strength in the new positions your body obtains through increased mobility.

A higher box height will allow for an overload from the parallel box and a lower box height will under load the parallel box squat.

Make sure you set the box back far enough that you will not trip over it, but close enough so that you can sit on it without falling backwards off balance.

Box Squat

Purpose

- **Teach Proper Squatting Mechanics**
- **Test Lower Body Strength**
- **Build Leg and Core Strength**

Prime Movers

- **Quadriceps** (Legs)
- **Hamstrings** (Legs)
- **Glutes** (Hips)

Set-Up

Grab The Bar

Grasp bar firmly, with thumbs wrapped, as close to your shoulders as you can while maintaining a relatively neutral wrist position, that allows you to still pull the bar into your body.

If you grab too wide, then you will lose back tightness and risk falling out of position. If you grab too close, then you can stress your wrists and will be pushing the bar off your back rather than creating tightness from it.

Find the best position for you, and if you have shoulder or wrist mobility problems you should try to improve them before every training session. You can do this with my *How To Warm-Up Guide*.

Set Your Feet Directly Under The Bar

Set your feet directly under the bar in your squat stance so that the bar is directly over your mid foot.

If you set your feet behind the bar, then you will waste valuable energy as you have to pull the weight out of the rack from in front of your center of gravity.

You want to be able to stand straight up with the weight and not be out of position.

Set The Bar On Your Back

Squat down and place the bar in the strongest position for you on your upper back, anywhere between the base of your neck and middle of rear deltoids (shoulder muscle).

Note: *A higher bar position will emphasize greater knee flexion and less torso lean, while a lower bar position will emphasize more torso lean and less knee flexion.*

Unrack

Brace Your Core

Suck in as much air as you can and hold it in, attempting to create as much intra-abdominal pressure as you can, to stabilize your spine. Then press your lips closed to hold the air in while flexing all of the musculature surrounding your entire torso, and forcing the air deep down into your abdomen. This is known as the Valsalva Maneuver.

Hold this tightness throughout your entire set-up.

Pull The Bar Into You

Pull your elbows down and in towards your hips throughout the movement, as if you are going to bend the bar over your back. This keeps that bar locked in and it should never, ever slide out of place, if done properly.

Push Your Head Back Into The Bar

While keeping a neutral spine, force your head back into the bar, with your eyes straight ahead. Imagine pulling your chin straight back, and never tilt your head up.

Maintain a neutral head position (straight spine) throughout the entire lift with eyes straight ahead.

Stand Straight Up With The Weight

Flex your glutes hard as you simultaneously, extend your knees and hips to lift the bar straight up, just over the rack hooks. Stay tight while you do this.

Walk It Out

Slide one foot at a time back 3-4 inches, or just enough to clear the rack hooks, so you are standing in your squat stance.

The farther you move the more likely you are to be out of position and waste energy. The bar should move straight up and down when you squat, so you do not need to move back very far.

FOOT POSITION

Toes should point somewhere between 10-45 degrees out depending on your stance width and mobility. Try different positions and see what works best for you.

If your heels come up as you squat or you have trouble getting to depth, then try either turning your toes out more or widening your stance, until you improve your ankle mobility.

GRAB THE GROUND

Suction cup your feet to the ground by spreading your toes as wide as you can, then grasping the floor with your entire foot. Your entire foot (heel, ball of your foot, and outer edge) should stay locked into the ground.

Then, while clenching your toes into the ground like eagle claws, create torque by externally rotate your feet, as if they were to spin in place, throughout the entire motion.

This movement should flex your entire lower body from your glutes down through your entire legs so that everything is tight, and nothing is loose or relaxed.

Maintain this external rotation torque throughout the lift.

Note: *By grabbing the ground with your foot you are simply creating a strong arch in your foot, not rolling your ankle. Your feet should not move out of place or come up at all during these motions. Just create a rotational pressure to stabilize your joints, while your entire foot is locked into the ground.*

Re-Brace Your Core

While keeping your entire body tight, again suck in as much air as you can and press it down deep into your abdomen increasing the intra-abdominal pressure. Hold this tightness throughout the entire lift.

Bend At The Hip

Initiate the motion by bending at the waist, pushing your hips back slightly, maintaining a neutral spine as if doing a 3 inch bow. This is a slight motion just to open the hips.

The weight should stay over your mid foot, with no back arching.

Push Your Knees Out

Push your knees out laterally to open your hips throughout the lift. This better engages your hips and makes for a stronger squat.

Your knees should travel in line with your toes during the entire lift. If they cave in at all then you need to work on your glute strength AND adductor mobility (inner thigh - being able to do the splits better to open up your hips).

Control Your Squat Onto The Box

While maintaining a neutral spine, open your hips and descend back and down bending your knees and hips simultaneously until your hips set softly on the box. DO NOT DROP ONTO THE BOX! Control the entire movement!

While maintaining tightness in your legs and torso, pause on the box for at least 1-2 seconds before forcefully press back up into the bar as you ascend.

Press your knees out and curling your heels into the ground, extending your hip and knees together.

Keep your head neutral and knees out over your foot.

Key Points

- ☑ Stay tight throughout the entire set-up and squat.
- ☑ Pull the bar into you.
- ☑ Grab the ground with your feet.
- ☑ Torque your knees out throughout the full range of motion.
- ☑ Control your squat, sitting onto the box softly.
- ☑ Maintain a neutral spine and head position.
- ☑ Drive back up into the bar to stand.

Always use spotters during your squats for safety.

How To Spot For Squats

You should always squat in a Power Rack if you have one available, with the safety bars set to where the bar is about 3 inches away from them at the base of your squat. This can help save your life if some freak accident happens or you fail a lift.

For those that do not have this safety rack to squat in, or if you are practicing what it is like to squat on the platform in open space, you should always use spotters. This can actually make you stronger no matter what weight you are using. Not stronger because they are assisting the lift, but stronger by encouragement and by the confidence of having others around you.

So, if you are not training with a friend or two, you should be! They will help keep you accountable as you both fight through the tough training. Plus, they will be there when you need them!

If you do go to the gym alone, don't worry. Getting a spot for any lift is quit easy. All you have to do is ask!

Don't be shy either. If they are too busy, let them tell you that. Don't assume that they do not want to help, because most gym goers would be honored that you feel confident in them to help you. Just make sure you take a moment to asses the gym for potential spotters, if you don't have any on hand, to make sure you pick the right ones.

The Spotter

First, let's discuss what a "spotter"is. A spotter is someone that helps promote safety of the lifter by assisting the lift in case of a failed attempt.

If the lifter does not fail a lift or ask for assistance, then the spotter SHOULD NOT TOUCH THE WEIGHT!!! If a spotter does touch the weight, no matter the amount of assistance given, the lift is considered a failed attempt.

Lifters should always use spotters, especially on lifts exceeding 80% of the lifters maximum and on sets in which the lifter gets close to failure.

Again, spotters are only there to assist in case the lifter fails. If the weight does not stop moving upward, then the spotter should not touch the weight, even if it is moving slowly.

All spotter assisted lifts DO NOT COUNT! Period! Exclamation point! Angry face!

Choosing Your Spotters

When choosing spotters, it is best to choose people that are focused on your safety. They don't have to be very strong, because they do not have to lift all the weight. They just have to lift the extra 5% you can't. Your grandmother can spot you if you want! They just have to be focused on the moment and not staring at the girl across the gym.

You don't need the biggest, strongest or most experienced person to help you out. They are no use if they are not paying attention to your lift, or distracted with their own workout. It is great to get people with a lot of experience, but it can also be really great to teach new people how to spot too.

Anyone can learn how to spot most lifts in a matter of seconds. Just explain what you are going to do and what you need them to do in case the worst happens. If they can understand what to do and be focused on the moment, then they are perfect! It can even be a great learning experience for them if they have not done it much before.

There are 3 ways to spot for the squat:

1. **Back Spot** - most common, but not very safe for anyone.
2. **Side Spots** - very safe and highly recommended.
3. **Back and Side Spots** - most safe and preferred above all else if possible.

How To Back Spot

A Back Spotter is someone that squats directly behind you and lifts you up in case of a failed lift.

This spotter should stand close enough to quickly grab the lifter in a split second if needed, but far enough away that they do not touch the lifter in any way during the lift. There should be about 3-6 inches of clearance between the lifter and the back spotter's bodies during the entire lift.

The Back Spotter should stand with arms hooked under the lifter's armpits, with 3-6 inches of space away from the lifter, during the squat. If the lifter fails the lift, then the back squatter should hug onto the lifter, with hands on the lifter's chest, helping to guide the lifter up, NOT back.

If the back spotter pulls back on the lifter, they may pull the weight out of the lifter's center of gravity which will lead to the weight falling on the back spotter, likely causing major injury.

This spotting method is common, because it only requires one spotter, but is not very safe.

How To Side Spot

A Side Spotter is someone that stands at each end of the barbell and lift the weight up in case of a failed lift.

This spotter should stand slightly in front of, or behind the weight plates on each side, close enough to grab the weights if needed. There can be up to 2 side spotters on each side of the barbell, but one on each side is most common.

The side spotter will need to squat with the weight, having one arm hooked under the end of the barbell or weights, with the other arm in front or behind the weight plates, leaving only 3-6 inches distance from grabbing the weight.

If the lifter fails the lift, it is very important the the side spotters lift the weight straight up with the lifter, and at the same speed as each other. You do not want one side coming up faster than the other making for a lopsided barbell.

Also, try to get spotters that are about the same height.

Having side spotters is very safe and I highly recommend you have them for all of your intense sets.

Back and Side Spots

A combination of both a back spotter and side spotters is the safest way to do your squats. This ensures that the lifter is taking all necessary precautions to lift as safely as possible.

The back and side spotters perform their spots the same as described above. In case of failure, the spotters will all be there to assist.

If for any reason the bar slips off of the squatter's back, all spotters should jump back away from the weight and not try to catch it. It is the squatter's job to stay with the bar and not risk the safety of everyone around them by dropping the bar.

Sometimes, things happen though.

You will see this style of spotting in all sanctioned powerlifting competitions and most powerlifting gyms that care for the lifter's safety. If you want to lift big numbers, this is the way to go with your spotters.

PART 3

BUILDING STRENGTH

12-WEEK SQUAT PROGRAM

Maximize Your Squat Strength!

This program is based on the Mathias Method Strength System.

12-weeks. 12-weeks of hard work. That is all it takes.

During that time you will be significantly improving your squat technique and building an incredible amount of strength. Both of which will have you more than ready to set a brand new PR!

However, it won't be easy. Over the next 12-weeks you will be taken on a journey that will lead you to something you have never done before. You will be pushed and tested every step of the way. You will learn new ways of building strength that you may have never learned otherwise and you will take your strength beyond what you may have ever imagined. When you are done, you will be changed and look back at where you used to be only to see how far you have come.

The only thing to do next is ask, "what's next?"! The answer, is up to you…

Note: *This is a 12-week cyclical program that is meant to be done over-and-over again for as long as you wish. After completing a cycle, you can immediately start back over at week 1. However, I recommend you take 1-2 weeks between cycles to just go into the gym and have some fun doing workouts with less strict programming. This will give you a mental break from the strict programming and help you come back refreshed and ready for the next 12-weeks.*

This Squat Program does not promise that you will achieve a 500+ lb squat in just 12-weeks. But I do guarantee that, if you put in the work, your strength will go up over-and-over again until you reach your full squatting potential! Whether that is 500+lbs or not is up to you!

Program Details

This is a 12 Week Strength Program that focuses on increasing your squat max. In it I will guide you through the exact work you need to do in order to reach your new Squat Max, and eventually to Squat 500+ lbs.!

This program can be used to repeatedly improve your squat until your reach your goal of squatting 300, 400 and even 500+ pounds! After you finish one 12 week phase, simply take a week off from squatting and then begin again!

For many, this program may seem like a lot, but to squat more than before you have to put in more work than before. You have to do hard things, because hard things make you stronger.

This program is best for lifters with at least a year of squatting experience under their belt. If you have not been practicing your squat for that long or more, then you will benefit more from my *Base Of Strength Training Program* (see page 6), which is made to help you improve all 3 of your main lifts, simultaneously.

This Program has 3 Phases:

1. **Volume Phase**
2. **Strength Phase**
3. **Max Phase**

Each Phase is 3 weeks long with every 4th week being a deload before starting the next phase.

Phase 1 - Volume

The first 3 weeks of your training is the Volume Phase. This Phase will focus on increasing your total work capacity with light to moderate weight and a lot of volume.

This is the time to improve your technique and reset your squat so that your body is ready for the more intense work ahead without becoming over fatigued.

This Volume Work is also used as a "Strength Reset" in which you give your body time off from maximal work to prepare it for more progress at your new found strength. This Phase is vital for your maximal strength, and will have your body craving more intense weights when complete.

Deload Weeks

Every 4th week in this program is a deload and recovery week. This week allows your body to catch up on recovery, build up other weak areas and prepare you for the high intensity workouts the following week.

This is the time to focus on other accessory lifts, that will help to build up your body's weak areas and improve your overall strength.

Your Main Lift for these weeks will be Box Squats, which were covered earlier in this book. Box Squats are a great variation to help perfect your squat technique and teach you to control the entire movement. Just remember not to drop on the box, but sit softly, pause, then explode up. This will build a tremendous amount of strength at the bottom of the squat.

If you want an even harder challenge, you can also switch these out for pause squats, where you do a normal squat, but pause at the bottom for 1-2 seconds, the same as you would for a box squat.

The intensity will be much lower on these weeks and you should not push yourself too hard. Just get in some work to improve your lift, but save most of your energy for the intense workout the following week.

Week 8 is another deload week, and is vital to allow your body enough time to recover fully before taking on your most intense workouts during your 4 week Peaking Phase!

Phase 2 - Strength

The next 3 weeks (5-7) are your Strength Phase. These workouts combine intensity and volume to build up the greatest amount of strength.

These workouts will be long and hard, but you will feel like a true Strength Warrior if you can get through them without being crushed by the weight!

Take your time with every set and make sure that you are moving with a purpose on every rep. Be in control of the weight, and do not let the weight take control of you.

Phase 3 - Max

The final 4 weeks, including your deload week, are what is called your Max Phase, or Peaking Phase. These workouts are designed to increase your maximal strength and prepare you to crush your peak week!

This is where you have your most intense workouts before backing off for at least 10-14 days in order to hit a Strength Peak where your body is ready to lift the most weight for your main lift.

These 4 weeks are crucial to nail perfectly in order to peak at the right time and get the greatest improvement in your squat max.

Make sure your recovery is on point and you do not do anything out of the ordinary during these 4 weeks.

Peak Week

Peak Week starts with your Week 11 - Workout 1 and goes until your Max Day.

You will start Week 11 by working up to the heaviest weight that you feel you can do 2-3 clean reps with. This should be at least 90% of your old maximum, but can also be well over your previous 100% max, depending on how well the program has worked for you so far. This is going to be your heaviest workout of the cycle, but it is not meant for you to do an all time max. This is still a preparation for your max day, so save some.

When you find your perfect weight, you are going to do 5-10 singles with it, stopping when form begins to break down too much. If form breaks down before you reach 5 reps then you need to significantly drop the weight to where you can do clean singles. If you are working into a competition, then this working weight should be your opening lift.

This workout should give you a good idea of what your max should be on max day. If this workout goes well, then you can expect to hit 110% of this weight on max day. For example, if you were able to do 5-10 good singles with 450 lbs. then you can expect to squat 500+ lbs. on max day.

This is your last heavy workout before you max and you should plan to max 10-14 days after this workout.

You will finish Week 11 off with your normal Base Work before moving to week 12.

Week 12 is also a deload week in which you will do minimal work and very low intensity for all of your lifts, so that your body is more than ready for Max Day.

You will start the week by doing only 5 sets of 1-3 reps at 50% of your max for both Squats and Deadlifts, followed by your normal Accessory Work. Keep your accessory work light and easy on this day and just get some movement in. You do not want to take the week off from lifting, but you also do not want to fatigue yourself with any of your workouts.

Keep all your workouts light and easy this week and have at least 1-3 days off from all training before max day.

MAX DAY

Max Day is your day. It is the day you have prepared for with every workout over the past 12 weeks. You are ready for this and you should wake up feeling super human!

Make sure that you are fully rested on the days leading up to your Max Day and your nutrition is on point. Stay hydrated and eat normally.

Do not try any new supplements or food protocols around this day. You don't need to be overly stuffed or caffeinated to lift heavy. You have been preparing for weeks and you are ready. Just go do it.

Take your time on Max Day. Take your time waking up. Take your time eating before hand. Take your time getting to the gym and take your time warming up. This is your day so let it last.

Warm-up slowly and take as long as you need between sets. As you get over 80% your rest should be between 5-10 minutes, not more or less.

Make sure everything is feeling good and move violently. If the weight is light, then it should look light. Drive into every rep as if it is your max and make sure your body is prepared to be explosive with that new max.

If you prepared properly, then this day will be easy for you.

When you are ready, go for it! Be confident in yourself and show the world WHO YOU ARE!!! It's Game Time! Go dominate!

Remember to tag @MathiasMethod when you post your new PR so I can see how you did!

If you want some good Game Day Motivation, then check out my motivation book *Motivated Mindset* (see page 6)! It will get you fired up for anything you pursue in your life no matter the challenges you face!

How To Max Out Properly

How you work up to your max can greatly effect your maximal strength. The goal is to stimulate your body for a maximal lift without over-fatiguing yourself to where you have major strength loss.

If you go in and do a bunch of unnecessary reps you are just going to be waisting energy. It is better to do more sets and less reps to conserve energy than try to do a full workout before hand. You wouldn't run a mile to warm up for a sprint, so don't make the same mistake here. All you need to do is feel the weight. When the weight feels good, move up.

Below we give you a common max out protocol, but you can add more sets if needed. Remember, the goal is to get your body prepared for maximal weight, and not fatigue you.

Take your time between sets and go when you are ready keeping the reps low. Remember to be explosive with every single rep as if it is a maximal lift.

How To Work Up To Your New Max:

- **Bar x 5-10**
- **30-40% x 5-10**
- **50-60% x 3-5**
- **70-75% x 3**
- **80-85% x 1-3**
- **90-95% x 1**
- **100-105% x 1**
- **105%+ x 1**

Add multiple sets as needed.

All percentages are based on your projected max calculated by your Week 11 - Workout 1 working weight multiplied by 110%. If you used 450 lbs. as your working weight for all 5-10 singles, then your projected max is 500 lbs.

If you had to lower the weight for that workout, then use the lower weight to calculate your projected max.

It is better to warm-up a little lighter than it is to warm-up going too heavy.

Weekly Workout Schedule

This squat program has you squatting 2 times per week. Workout 1 is your Strength Work in which you will be improving your squat's maximal strength through intense training. Workout 2 is your Base Work in which you will be practicing your technique and increasing your overall training volume.

Your first workout of the week should focus on the lift you want to improve. In this case, that is your squat. Make sure that you have at least 1 rest day before this training day, in which you do no gym or cardio work. That will allow you to be the most fresh and prepared to take on the challenging workout ahead.

The second squat workout of the week should occur 3-4 days after your first squat workout. It would also be best to have a recovery day before this training day, but it is not required. Just make sure that you are recovering enough.

All other workouts throughout the week should not include squats of any kind. Avoid fatiguing your legs on other training days, but you can use any training split you want.

This is the training split we have found most effective for this training program.

Day 1 - **Squat Workout 1** (Strength Work)

Day 2 - Off

Day 3 - Bench Press Workout 1

Day 4 - Off

Day 5 - **Squat Workout 2** (Base Work)

Day 6 - Bench Press Workout 2

Day 7 - Off

On all of your other training days, make sure that you do not push yourself too hard. If improving your squat is your main focus, then save most of your energy for your squat days. Just get the work in that you need for other lifts and muscle groups to stay strong. Doing a 5x5 workout at about 70% with small 5lb. jumps every week should be enough to keep your other main lifts moving forward without over stressing your body. Or get my *Bench BIG Program* (see page 6) to pair with this one!

Do not deadlift on any other training days, either. Save it for your squat days.

#MathiasMethod #Squat500

Follow @MathiasMethod on Social Media
and tag us in your #Squat500 workout clips!

Also, feel free to reach out anytime with your questions or technique checks!

SQUAT WORKOUTS

STRENGTH WORK

The first workout of each week is your "Strength Work" in which you will focus on building maximal strength. This workout will have the heaviest lifts of the training week and require the most preparation and recovery.

Over the 12 weeks the intensity will vary to allow for optimal recovery between high intensity training sessions.

The first 3 weeks will have a gradual progression as you increase your work capacity and prepare for the high demanding work load ahead. Then every 4th week is a deload week in which you will take a break from the intense lifting and work on other accessory lifts. This is the time where you can do a light variation of your main lift and work on a weak area.

The following weeks the intensity will vary between high and moderate each week as you gradually increase your total work load up until peak week.

Peak week is the last 10-14 days before your maximal lift attempt, starting with your first workout of week 11. It is crucial that you do this properly to get maximum results.

For your Maximal Work on week 11 you will work up to the heaviest weight you feel that you can do for about 2-3 reps, but make sure that you only do 1 rep. This should be at least 90%, but can also be well over your previous 100% max, depending on how well the program has worked for you so far. You are going to do 5-10 perfect singles with this weight, stopping only when you cannot perform the squat with reasonable form. Be careful not to push yourself too hard in this workout. You want to work hard, but not get injured before your max day.

After doing 5 or more singles with this weight, you can add a little weight, but no more than 3-5% if you feel good. If it is getting heavy during your first 5 singles, then maintain the same weight until form breaks down.

Week 12 is your official peak week in which you use very light weight and just work on the movement. You want to stretch out the movement, and allow for blood flow, but focus on recovery above all else.

Then, 4-7 days later test out your max by gradually working up in weight. Make sure that you get plenty of rest this week and only max out on a day that you feel ready, and not fatigued. Your other workouts during this week should also be light and easy.

Base Work

The second workout of each week is your Base Work. This is a light to moderately intense workout to help you get in more work while improving your technique.

For your Base Work you will be doing at least 5 sets of 5 reps with gradually increasing intensity. Most of the time you will be given a 5% range to work in. For this, work up to a weight within the range that feels good and moves well.

How you feel during these workouts will vary every week, so do not worry so much about the weight, even if you have to go lighter than expected. It is more important to focus on moving well and with perfect technique. Save the heavy stuff for your Strength Work days. Think of it as a movement and recovery workout.

As for your technique, since the weights are lighter for these workouts, every rep should be explosive and done with perfect form. Do not take it easy just because it is light. If it is light, then you should make it look easy by driving the weight up hard with every rep.

Also, for these workouts, only use equipment (belt, sleeves, wraps, etc.) if needed. Try to do every set 100% RAW, if you can. This will help increase your RAW strength and make you that much stronger when you do use equipment on other days.

Week 12 you will not have any Base Work as you prepare for Max Day. Use this as a recovery day.

PROGRAM CHART

WORKOUT 1 - STRENGTH WORK

WEEK	MAIN LIFTS	SETS	REPS	% MAX
1	Squat	5	5	70%
	Deadlift	4	6	55-60%
2	Squat	5	5	73%
	Deadlift	4	6	55-60%
3	Squat	5	5	75%
	Deadlift	4	6	55-60%
4	Box Squat	5	5	70%
	Deadlift	4	8	50-55%
5	Squat	8	3	80%
	Deadlift	4	6	60-65%
6	Squat	6	4	77%
	Deadlift	4	6	60-65%
7	Squat	6	2	85%
	Deadlift	4	6	60-65%
8	Box Squat	5	3	75%
	Deadlift	4	8	55-60%
9	Squat	5	2	87%
	Deadlift	4	5	65-70%
10	Squat	6	3	80%
	Deadlift	4	5	65-70%
11	*Squat	5-10	1	*90% +
	Deadlift	4	5	65-70%
12	Squat	5	3	50%
	Deadlift	5	1	50%

WORKOUT 2 - BASE WORK

WEEK	MAIN LIFT	SETS	REPS	% MAX
1	Squat	5	10	50%
2	Squat	5	10	55%
3	Squat	5	8	60%
4	Squat	5	5	65%
5	Squat	5	5	65-70%
6	Squat	5	5	65-70%
7	Squat	5	5	65-70%
8	Squat	5	5	70-75%
9	Squat	5	5	70-75%
10	Squat	5	5	70-75%
11	Squat	5	5	65-70%
12	**Squat**	***Max Day***		

***Week 11** - DO NOT MAX! Use the heaviest weight you can do 2-3 reps with for all 5-10 sets.

- **Weeks 1-4, 6, 8 and 10 (Workout 1) -** AMRAP the last set of squats using the same working weight. AMRAP = As Many Reps As Possible *(always leave 1-2 reps in the tank).*

- **Weeks 5, 7 and 9 (Workout 1) -** Work up to a Daily Max of 1-3 reps after all your squat sets are complete. Work up slowly taking as many sets as needed, but do not reach failure. Just move something heavy. If the weights did not move well during your sets, then just do an AMRAP for your last set with your working weight instead.

- **DO NOT change your weights after achieving a new max during the program -** Depending on your experience level, you may very well surpass your old max when doing your daily maxes. This is expected and accounted for in the programming. Do not change anything.

- **Week 11 -** DO NOT MAX OUT! Read the "Peak Week" section for details.

- **Always AMRAP the last set of squats on Base Work days.**

All percentages are based on your current max before beginning the program, not your projected max at the end.

Base your deadlift max on your belt-less max, as most if not all of your deadlifts will be done without a belt to help build up your core strength.

If you do not know your max, then do a low estimate. As in, something you know you can do 2-3 good reps with at the start of the program. You will actually get more out of the program if you go a little lighter than you need too versus going a bit too heavy.

Workout 1 - Strength Work

Warm-Up:

The Daily 30	1-3 Rounds
Weighted Pull-Ups	- x 25 total
Box Jumps (optional)	3-5 x 3

Technique Work:

Pause Squat (<50%)	3 x 5

Main Lifts:

Squat	See Program Chart
*Overload Set	See Program Chart Notes
Deadlift	See Program Chart

Accessory Work:

Leg Press / Glute-Ham Raises	5-10 x 10-15
Dumbbell Rows	5 x 6-8
Hammer Curls	4 x 8-10
Side Planks	3 x 45 sec.

Mobility Work	10+ min.

*Done after your main work is complete, and never to failure.

Go to MathiasMethod.com for in-depth exercise descriptions.

WORKOUT 2 - BASE WORK

Warm-Up:

The Daily 30	1-3 Rounds
Pull-Ups	- x 30-50

Technique Work:

Pause Squat (<50%)	3 x 5

Main Lift:

Squat	See Program Chart

Accessory Work:

Leg Curls	5 x 10-15
Lat Pull-Downs	5 x 10-15
Dumbbell Curls	3 x 10-15
Weighted Planks	3 x 30-60 sec.
Mobility Work	10+ min.

Go to MathiasMethod.com for in-depth exercise descriptions.

Workout Details

All workouts and training protocols follow the Mathias Method Strength System Principles.

In the Mathias Method Strength System we don't train muscle groups. We train movements and base our workouts on improving one lift. This is because lifts like the squat, bench press, and deadlift are all full body lifts. They take your entire body working in unison to perfect and do not target one specific area.

By building up these powerful compound movements we will develop strength and muscle throughout our entire body.

We also believe in using only the most effective accessory exercises. Big bang exercises that build big muscle and big strength. Yeah, they are hard ones and they make you brutally strong too.

This training style may be different than what you are used to, but it is what has worked for me and countless others with the same goal of getting brutally strong.

The details of your training are discussed below.

The Warm-Up

Warm-ups are just what you think. They are simply meant too, warm-up your body for the intense work ahead, not overly fatigue you.

If you are not used to doing some warm-up exercises before your main work, then it will be fatiguing at first until your body gets more conditioned. This is part of developing the work capacity to lift heavy weight, so do not skip this just because you do not feel like it. If you want to get stronger, you're gonna have to put in the work no matter how you "feel".

Warm-ups should be relatively easy and never done to failure.

Every workout you do should start with 1-3 rounds of *The Daily 30* (see page 6) to practice your movement patterns and improve mobility while you warm-up. This may seem unnecessary, but it will do wonders for your strength and help to alleviate any muscle or joint pain you have.

For both training days you will also warm-up with pull-ups. Back strength is actually one of the most important factors in providing strength for all of your lifts, which is why we have you start every workout with pull-ups to develop back strength.

If you can't do pull ups then you can use a band for assistance or replace these with heavy lat pull-downs, but if you've been training for a while you know that there really is no replacement for pull-ups. They are a vital exercise that our bodies were designed to do and need to be practiced often. They decompress your spine and build back strength like nothing else can!

You can do these with your hands facing in (chin-ups - bicep focused) or facing away (pull-ups - Lat focused) as you desire.

Do as many sets as it takes to get to the set number of reps, never going to failure.

For weighted pull-ups you want to aim for a weight that allows you to do 5 sets of 5 reps or so. Adjust the weight as needed.

If you cannot do 10 pull-ups in a row, then either do heavy lat pull-down for 5x10 on your Base Work training days or cut the reps down to 30 total for those workouts.

As part of your warm up on Strength Work days you can also include plyometrics. This is optional, but highly recommended.

Plyometrics have an incredible ability to prepare your body for maximal lifts through the reflexive contraction that they provide, very similar to a maximal squat. The key is to jump to a difficult height onto a box, but not so high that you risk missing the box. Then slowly over time try to increase the height. As the box height raises, so too will your squat max!

For added strength and performance, follow my How To Warm-Up Guide (see page 6) before every workout!

Technique Work

Exercise Technique is a crucial part of any movement based training program. Without proper technique your body will learn improper movement patterns that can hold back your strength and cause injury.

Technique is so important that it should be checked and improved every time you start a training session!

Your technique work is still part of your warm-up and therefore only light weights (<50% of your maximum) should be used to prevent over fatiguing yourself. The focus is on improving your movement pattern by utilizing perfect form, under controlled movements.

To develop more strength at the bottom of the squat we will use pause squats as your technique warm-up before every squat session. You will simply do a squat as normal, pause at the bottom for 2 seconds, then explode back up without losing positioning.

The main goals of this exercise is to prepare your body for the more intense work ahead, build up weaknesses and increase work capacity.

You should do only 3 sets of 5 perfect reps. Again, the goals are to improve the motion of this exercise and better prepare your body for the work ahead, not to pre-fatigue those muscles.

After completing your Technique Work, you are ready to begin your workout!

Start with your first exercise by doing the same number of repetitions you plan to train with for that day. If you are doing 3 reps for your working sets, do all your warm-ups with 3 reps. Start with a low intensity and work your way up slowly.

The Main Lift

The main lift, or main lifts, of any given workout, is the focus point of the session, where you put in the most effort. All of the training before and after the main lift is set to better improve this movement.

As this book is all about how to improve your squat max, squats will always be your main lift for both workouts. One day per week they will be done at a high intensity with low reps to build maximal strength, while one day per week they will be done with a light-moderate intensity as you accumulate volume and practice technique, creating a higher potential for strength gain.

Together, varying between light, moderate and heavy loads will allow for continuous growth without stagnation.

Follow the 12 Week Squat Program Chart for your squat sets, reps and intensity.

Always warm-up to your working weight slowly during each workout to fully prepare yourself for the work ahead.

Overload Sets

Overload sets are part of your Main Lift work on Strength Work training days. For this you will either do an AMRAP (as many reps as possible) set or work up to a Daily Max.

AMRAP

Weeks 1-4, 6, 8 and 10 - AMRAP the last set of squats using the same working weight.

For your AMRAP sets, do as many reps as possible minus one. We always minus one because we do not want to ever risk failure. It is better to save some for later, then grind with bad form or risk missing a lift, which stalls progress.

Daily Max

Weeks 5, 7 and 9 - Work up to a Daily Max of 1-3 reps after all your squat sets are done.

A Daily Max is a near maximum lift for that given day. It is not a true maximum, because you are fatigued from all the previous work.

For your Daily Max, work up to something heavy, but do not push so hard that you lose technique or risk failure.

Depending on your experience level, you may very well surpass your old max when doing your daily maxes. This is expected and accounted for in the programming. Do not change anything.

DO NOT do any overload sets on weeks 11-12!

Main Accessory Work

Your main accessory is the main accessory lift that directly helps improve your main lift. This lift is included on the 12 Week Squat Program Chart and is only done on your Strength Work training days.

For squats your main accessory is the deadlift.

In any program, you can't talk about squats without talking about deadlifts, and you can't talk about deadlift without talking about squats. These two lifts work hand in hand to benefit each other. That is why we programmed for both lifts.

For your main accessory deadlifts, you can do any variation that best helps to improve your squat strength. This can vary every workout or be the same during all 12 weeks. I recommend conventional deadlift because it builds more core and hip strength, but sumo stance will still work well.

The idea for this lift is not to overly fatigue you beyond recovery, but rather just hit your muscles from a different angle to stimulate new growth. Just get in some work and do not push too hard. You already did your main strength work. Work the motion with moderate weight and then move on.

Accessory Work

Your accessory work is just a few hard hitting exercises to help build more strength and muscle throughout your entire body. You will be pretty exhausted by this point, but push through and take it as a mental challenge that will make you even stronger.

Your accessory work should be performed with moderate-intensity to allow for optimal muscle growth and proper technique. Always maintain good form to ensure proper muscle activation throughout the entire lift.

Focus on stimulating the muscle rather than just throwing around tremendous weight. It is important to always be in control of the weight.

Work every exercise hard and try to move up in weight when you can.

Make sure to finish off with some mobility work to prevent injury.

Strength Workouts

The accessory work for your Strength Work starts off with 5-10 sets of either leg press or glute-ham raises. You can switch between each of these week to week, or just focus on improving one each cycle.

If you have weak quads, its best you choose leg press. Do 5-10 hard sets with moderate to heavy weight and really push your legs to build as much quad strength as possible. If you do not have a leg press, then you can do front squats or a similar quad focused squat movement instead.

If you have weak hamstrings, then it is best you choose glute-ham

Raises. This is one of the most effective exercises for building brutally strong hamstrings that can support huge lifts. If you cannot perform these properly I recommend you start with controlled negative reps (lower yourself slowly) until you build the strength to do reps on your own.

You can start by kneeling on a pad and having a friend sit on your ankles and descend slowly under control before doing a push up to press yourself back up. When you get strong enough to do these without assistance, your lifts will likely have shot up significantly by now and you can start holding a weight plate across your chest.

If you do not have a gute-ham raise at your gym, or a friend to help out, you can just do some heavy leg curls instead, but it just won't give you the same results.

Next you will move onto heavy dumbbell rows. Feel free to use straps on these in order to grip heavier weight, but only go as heavy as you can while maintaining proper form. Then pick any bicep curl variation you like before moving onto some side planks and finishing with some mobility work to keep your body injury free.

Base Workouts

For your Base Work accessories you start off with leg curls to counter balance all the quad work you just got from volume squats. Then you will finish you back work with lat pull-downs before moving onto some curls and weighted planks.

If you are having knee pain it is likely due to your quads overpowering your hamstrings so do some light leg curls at the start of your workouts for extra accessory work to build up your hamstring strength.

Cardio/Conditioning

Conditioning, or cardio, is not necessary for this program, but can assist with dropping weight and improving recovery, if needed. Just DO NOT do cardio to warm-up!

Conditioning, is any form of work that improves your cardiovascular health and total work capacity while assisting with the goals of training. Some examples of conditioning are; jogging, sprints, jump rope, battle ropes, light circuit training, a daily WOD, sled dragging, or just manual labor.

Conditioning is meant to increase the ability for your body to withstand work and become stronger. If you have low cardiovascular health and little muscular endurance then the amount of work your body can withstand is greatly diminished, along with your ability to become stronger. So, if you have a low work capacity, you should add in conditioning until it improves.

Conditioning can be performed 2-4 times per week for 10-20 minutes at a time. You may utilize high intensity interval training (HIIT) or moderate intensity steady state training.

With high intensity intervals, work to rest should be at a 1:1 or 1:2 ratio. For moderate intensity steady state conditioning, the body should stay in motion throughout the entire time with little to no resistance in order to sustain a raised heart rate during the time used.

It is best to do conditioning immediately after all accessory work, just before mobility work. This will add to the work already done in the workout and allow for the greatest increase in muscular advancement.

Conditioning can also be done on non-training days if preferred, but should then be done for 20-30 minutes. Remember, conditioning is meant to condition your body, not break it down beyond what your body can repair before the next training session. Use relatively light loads and just keep moving.

Mobility Work

Mobility Work is 10+ minutes of stretching at the end of every workout used increase flexibility, prevent injury and improve recovery. Focus on stretching out the muscle you just worked, or other tight areas.

It can be as simple as doing just 2-3 stretches for 2 minutes each to fix your elbow, shoulder, ankle, or hip pain.

Mobility work can also be replaced by yoga or any other activity that improves your body's ability to move as intended without pain, such as rolling out soft tissues.

It is best to mobilize right after a workout, but it can also be done on non-training days.

The goal is to get at least 30-40 minutes of mobilization done weekly to enhance your recovery and performance. That is just 10 minutes 3-4 times per week.

Rest Periods

Rest periods between sets will vary for each part of the workout.

During your warm-up you can superset all your exercises together, as the intensity is not very high for these exercises, or you can take your time with each exercise to prevent fatiguing yourself too much before your main work. It is your warm-up, so do what works best for you.

For all your squats, or main lifts, rest as long as you need between sets, but realize that the longer you take between sets, the longer the workout will last due to the numerous sets.

Typically rest should be 2-3 minutes for loads less than 75% of your maximum and 3-5 minutes for anything heavier. You can take longer if needed, but don't waste all your time waiting to be ready. It is supposed to be hard and tiring, so push yourself and improve your conditioning if needed.

For all accessory work, rest 1-2 minutes between sets.

Training To Failure

There are 2 types of failure in training; technical and absolute.

- **Technical failure** is the point in which you can no longer perform a repetition with reasonably perfect technique. This commonly occurs 1-2 repetitions before absolute failure.
- **Absolute failure** is when no more repetitions can be completed without assistance.

It is good to know what failure feels like, but most of your work should be done with reasonably perfect technique to build the most optimal amount of strength.

You should really only reach technical failure on the last 1-2 sets of any workout, if at all. This means you reached maximal stimuli of the muscle fibers and central nervous system while still performing safe technique.

Reaching absolute failure too often will result in a much greater chance for injury and a much longer recovery period that may extend beyond the next training session. Not only that, but it teaches improper lifting technique as your body fights to lift the weight, and makes you weaker in the long run.

If you are training to failure, then you are training to fail!

The idea for strength training is too, accumulate volume for growth over multiple training sessions per week utilizing perfect practice. This will ensure safety while gaining the most amount of strength over time.

If You Do Fail

In training, your squats should never go beyond technical failure during this entire program, excluding your Max Day. However, if you ever do fail a rep, then drop the weight by 10% multiplied by the number of reps you have left in your set and do the rest of your sets in shame.

For example, if you failed your last rep, then take off only 10%. If you failed on your 4th rep out of 5, then take off 20%.

If you complete the rest of your sets at this new weight with good form, then you can go back up in weight, but this decreased percentage is your punishment for not recovering properly. Shame on you! Just don't blame me for your lack of preparation.

Also, if the weight is effecting your technique too much and you are moving slow or out of position, then drop the weight by 10-20% until it looks better. It is your job to lift the weight properly and if you cannot do that, then your punishment is lifting lighter weight until you can get it right. Again, not my fault. Just do it right and make it look easy!

Final Notes

- Things are going to go awry and that is ok. Not everything is going to go exactly as planned, and it will take time to perfect your squat technique no matter your experience level. Just be patient.

- Just like anything else, whenever you try something new, such as changing your squat technique, it will likely feel worse. Your body does not like change and the greater the change the worse things may feel. However, after practicing the new technique you will become so much stronger in the long run. Just trust in the technique and trust in the program. Practice and you will become perfect!

- Don't train lazy! If you do, you will develop bad habits that will haunt you for the rest of your lifting career! Don't squirm when you Bench, sit off to the side when you squat or shrug your deadlifts up. Make sure every rep is absolutely perfect and it will help you during your entire lifting career.

- Recovery is the most important thing! It doesn't matter what you do in the gym; if you can't recover from it, then you are not going to progress. Recovery is the only thing that is going to hold you back from making this program a success. So make sure you are getting enough sleep and fuel! That part is on you.

- Make sure you are doing your *Daily 30* to help with recovery and mobility throughout the entire program.

- Email me (ryan@mathiasmethod.com) with any questions!

- One more thing…

Would You Do Me A Favor?

Thank you for reading and I hope you learned a lot!

Before you go, please do me a HUGE favor and take a moment to let me know what you liked most about this book by leaving a review on Amazon! I read all my reviews and I love hearing how my work has helped others.

Plus, it helps more people learn what they can get from this book!

If you were not completely satisfied with the content of this book please let me know by emailing me directly and I will be happy to answer your questions or help you further.

Thank you, and keep getting stronger my friends!

Email: ryan@mathiasmethod.com

Do you know someone that would benefit from this book?

Please tell them about it!

Everyone can benefit from getting stronger!

More Books By Ryan J. Mathias

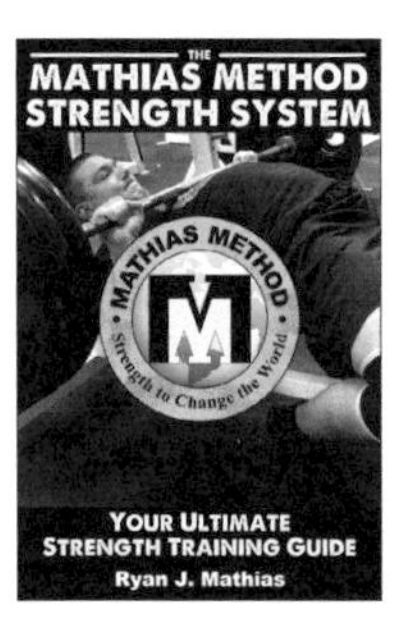

Available on

Amazon.com

and

StrengthWorld.store

FOLLOW US ON SOCIAL MEDIA

Facebook: @MathiasMethodStrength

Instagram: @MathiasMethod

Twitter: @MathiasMethod

YouTube: @MathiasMethodStrength

Reddit: u/mathiasmethod

Follow The Strength Blog

We have over 200+ articles on how to get stronger and workout properly, in and out of the gym!

Go to MathiasMethod.com to follow the Strength Blog and get all the awesome NEW Content we put out!

- **New Articles**
- **Workout Programs**
- **Valuable Strength Training Resources!**

Special Thank You

Ironworks Gym

153 South Auburn St.

Grass Valley, CA 95945

PHONE #: (530) 272-9462

Home of the Mathias Method STRENGTH WARRIORS!

Thank you for allowing us to use your awesome facility to help make the world a stronger place!

Strength is only the beginning.

It is what you do with it next that really matters.

Made in United States
Troutdale, OR
07/02/2023